BUGS

Firefly

Lynn Kuntz

KIDHAVEN PRESS

An imprint of Thomson Gale, a part of The Thomson Corporation

THOMSON
GALE

Detroit • New York • San Francisco • San Diego • New Haven, Conn. • Waterville, Maine • London • Munich

THOMSON
★
GALE

© 2006 Thomson Gale, a part of The Thomson Corporation.

Thomson and Star Logo are trademarks and Gale and KidHaven Press are registered trademarks used herein under license.

For more information, contact
KidHaven Press
27500 Drake Rd.
Farmington Hills, MI 48331-3535
Or you can visit our Internet site at http://www.gale.com

ALL RIGHTS RESERVED.
No part of this work covered by the copyright hereon may be reproduced or used in any form or by any means—graphic, electronic, or mechanical, including photocopying, recording, taping, Web distribution or information storage retrieval systems—without the written permission of the publisher.

Every effort has been made to trace the owners of copyrighted material.

LIBRARY OF CONGRESS CATALOGING-IN-PUBLICATION DATA

Kuntz, Lynn, 1953–
  Firefly / by Lynn Kuntz.
     p. cm. — (Bugs)
  Includes bibliographical references.
  ISBN 0-7377-3132-X (hardcover : alk. paper)
  1. Fireflies—Juvenile literature. I. Title. II. Series.
  QL596.L28K88 2005
  595.76'44—dc22
                                        2005005146

Printed in The United States of America

CONTENTS

Chapter 1
Winking and Blinking — 5

Chapter 2
A Magnificent Change — 11

Chapter 3
Fireflies Bulk Up — 16

Chapter 4
Fireflies Twinkle Around the World — 21

Glossary — 27

For Further Exploration — 28

Index — 30

Picture Credits — 31

About the Author — 32

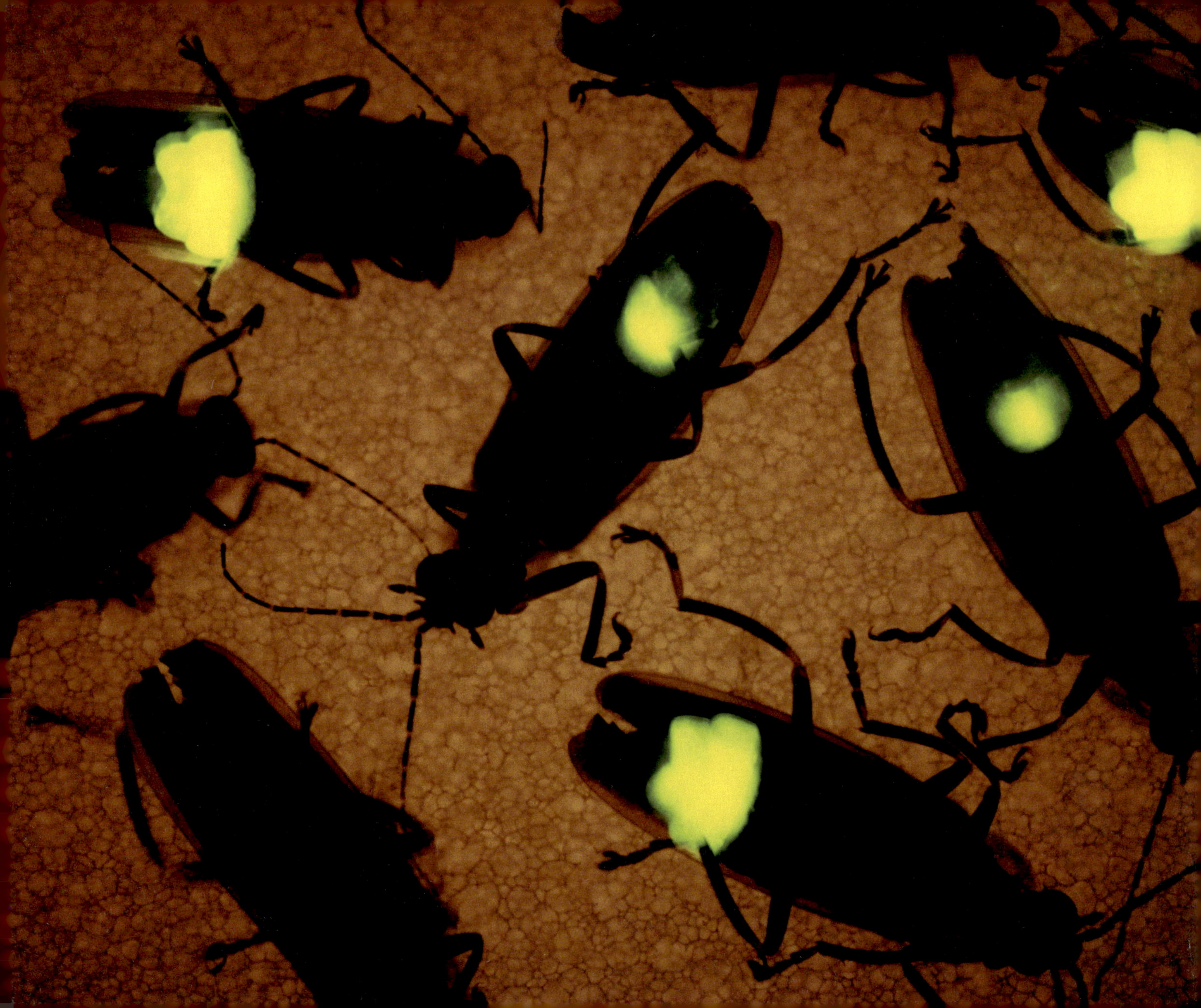

CHAPTER 1

Winking and Blinking

Fireflies are not really flies at all. They are soft-bodied, flying beetles with special light-making organs that glow in the dark. Curious scientists have been studying these creatures with their built-in flashlights for hundreds of years. They have identified more than 2,000 **species** of fireflies. Some shine at dusk, others at midnight. Some flash just one night per year. Some flash all year long.

Opposite: In this close-up view, the light organs of a group of fireflies flash brightly in the dark.

In this photo of a firefly resting on tree leaves, we clearly see the insect's outer wings, antennae, and six legs.

Body Parts

Adult fireflies have dark, narrow bodies, often marked with yellow, orange, or rosy pink streaks. They can measure from ¼ to 1¼ inches (5 to 30mm) long. A firefly's body, like that of all adult beetles, has three sections: the head, thorax, and abdomen.

The head features two **antennae**, a mouth with powerful **mandibles**, and two compound eyes. Fireflies depend on their antennae, which are sensitive to vibrations and smells, for information about their surroundings. Mandibles are curved, pincerlike, insect mouthparts used for biting, stabbing, and gripping. Compound eyes are made of many tiny eyes all joined together. Fireflies use their sight to find mates, so they have larger eyes than most beetles.

The thorax features six jointed legs and four wings. A stiff pair of outer wings, called the elytra, cover and protect the soft, inner wings that fireflies use for flying. During flight, the elytra are held open while the soft wings are flapped. The elytra behave like airplane wings, giving the firefly lift, while

Firefly

Body of a Firefly

Stiff outer wings protect the inner wings and provide lift during flight.

Antennae give the firefly information about its surroundings.

Sharp, pincerlike mandibles are used for biting, stabbing, and gripping.

The firefly uses its **large compound eyes** to find a mate.

Soft inner wings allow the insect to fly.

The firefly uses its **light organ** during mating and courting.

the inner wings provide the power. The females of some species are wingless.

The abdomen is where a firefly's sexual **organs** are and where females produce eggs. It is also where a firefly's light-producing organ is located and where food is digested. Fireflies even breathe from the abdomen, through tiny air holes called spiracles.

Every Twinkle Has a Time and Reason

Most fireflies are nocturnal, resting by day and **courting** and **mating** by night. The fireflies seen twinkling in nighttime skies are usually males, searching for females. When the male blinks his light organ, he is inviting a female to mate with him. His blinks and winks are in a secret code understood only by females of his particular species. A female, perched on a blade of grass close to the ground, can tell by the color of his light (green,

A male Jamaican firefly blinks his light organ in hopes of attracting a mate.

Firefly

yellow, or amber), its brightness, how long his flashes last, and the time between flashes that he belongs to her species. Her light organ is like a spotlight in the dark of night. He follows the spotlight until he finds her.

A Special, Living Light

Firefly light is called **bioluminescence**. *Bio* means "living." *Luminescence* means "light." Bioluminescence is "cold" light because a firefly wastes none of its energy making heat when it is making light. If a firefly's light was not a cold light, the firefly's flash would burn the firefly up. A firefly's bioluminescence is possible because of a chemical reaction that occurs when a rare chemical in the firefly's body, called **luciferin**, combines with a special enzyme in the firefly's body, called **luciferase**.

Thanks to its bioluminescence, the firefly is special and unique among all insects. The firefly's ability to glow is the feature that captures the imagination of people everywhere and makes the firefly possibly the best-loved insect in all the world.

A female firefly glows in order to guide her mate to her resting place on a blade of grass.

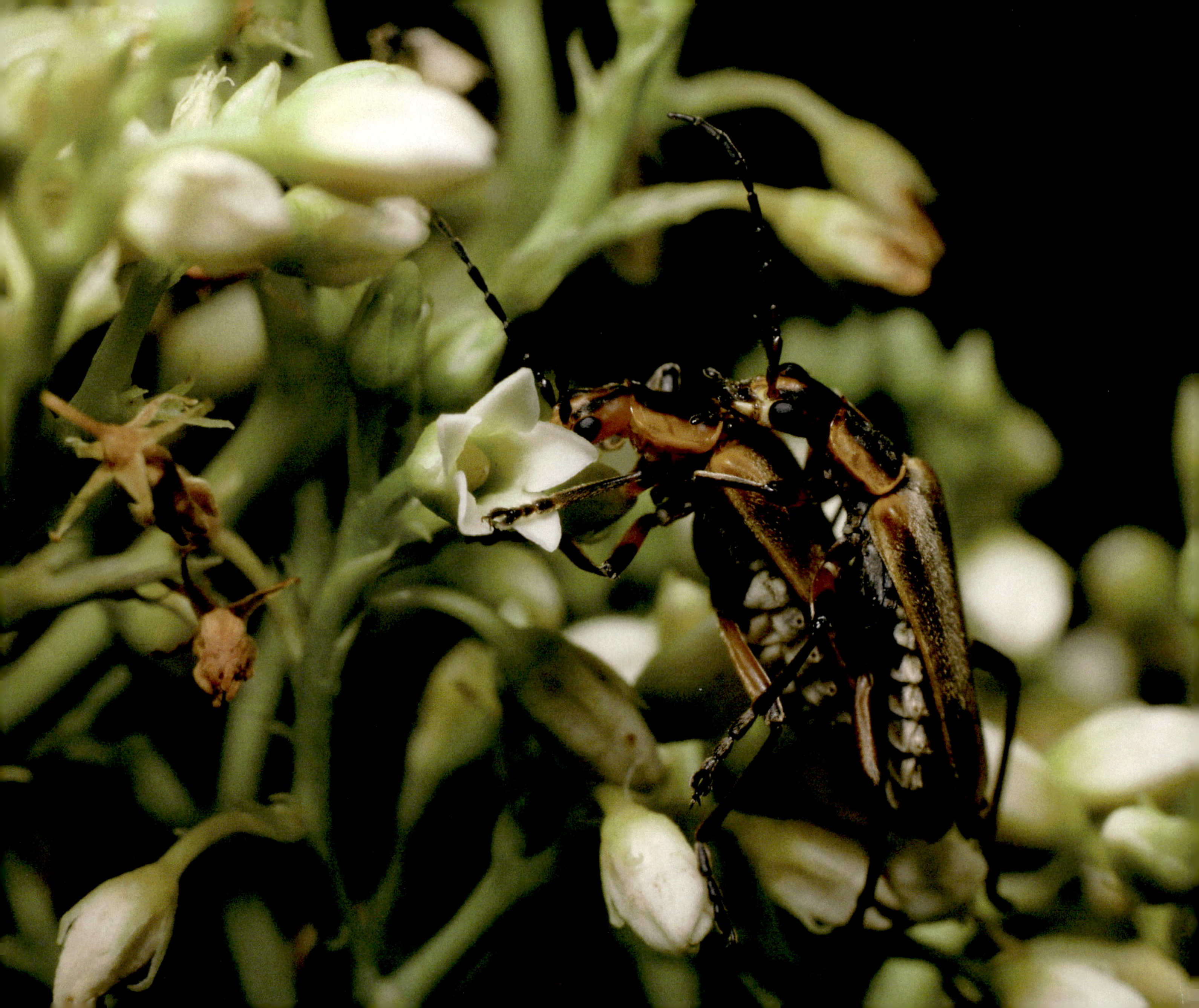

CHAPTER 2

A Magnificent Change

Like all beetles, fireflies go through a complete **metamorphosis**, or **transformation**, from the beginning to the end of their lives. This life **cycle** has four stages: egg, larva, pupa, and adult. The life cycle begins when a male and female come together and mate. Then the female lays up to a hundred tiny, round eggs in loose, moist soil. Each is the beginning of a new life.

Opposite: A pair of adult fireflies mates on the leaves and flowers of a bush.

Glowworms Are Not Really Worms

The eggs of most species glow softly in the dark. In just a few weeks, the eggs hatch into tiny, brown glowworms. Just as fireflies are not really flies, glowworms are not really worms. They are **luminous** (glowing) larvae—immature fireflies in the second, caterpillar stage of the life cycle.

Even though a newly hatched glowworm is not much bigger than the period at the end of this sentence, it already has eyes, antennae, a mouth with powerful, fanglike mandibles, six legs, and a small light organ on the underside of the abdomen. (For this reason, most glowworms must be turned

A glowworm hangs on a leaf as it sleeps.

upside down in order to see their glow.) It will spend most of its larval life eating as much as it possibly can by night and sleeping by day.

One Long Growth Spurt

A glowworm's job is to grow, grow, grow! Every so often, its expanding body outgrows its own, full-to-bursting skin. The old skin splits open and the glowworm grows new, larger skin several times during the larval stage. This is the longest stage of the firefly's life cycle. It may last from three months up to three years, with some species overwintering, or burrowing underground, for two or three winters before leaving the larval stage.

This glowworm, seen from its underside, glows in the dark as it rests on a fir tree.

A Magnificent Change 13

A fully mature glowworm prepares to turn into an adult firefly.

At last the glowworm is fully mature. Its instincts no longer urge it to find and eat food. Its new mission is to pupate—to turn into an adult firefly. The glowworms of some species attach themselves to bark by their rear ends and hang upside down to pupate. The glowworms of other species use body and legs, mandibles and mouth to dig into the moist soil and build underground, gumball-sized burrows where they will pupate. The glowworm's final larval skin splits open at just the right moment, revealing soft, pale pupal skin underneath. This new skin then hardens and darkens. Safe and quiet inside the caselike pupal skin, the final metamorphosis occurs.

The Fully Grown Firefly

The pupa's eyes begin to grow larger and its antennae much longer. Wings form in males and the females of some species. The tiny, built-in lantern grows into a larger and stronger light that is capable of flashing brightly. In days, weeks, or months, depending on the species, a fully grown, adult firefly will emerge from the pupal case, usually in early summer through late August.

Finally the firefly is ready to fulfill its purpose in life, which is to mate with another firefly and reproduce. After courtship and mating, a whole new cycle of life begins when the female lays her eggs.

When its final metamorphosis is complete, a fully grown firefly like this one emerges from the pupal case.

CHAPTER

3

Fireflies Bulk Up

The hungriest stage of a firefly's life is the larval stage. A glowworm may not look like a vicious attack animal, but firefly larvae are skilled, successful predators with enormous appetites. They feast on snails, slugs, worms, mites, insect larvae (including their fellow firefly larvae), and plant pollen.

When the sun goes down and many creatures go to sleep, glowworms wake up hungry and ready to hunt. Their sense of smell leads them to their prey. They are able to overpower living prey many times their size. They do this with two special weapons: deadly poisons they make in their bodies and their mandibles.

A glowworm's two mandibles are curved, like hooks, and sharp, like claws. A hollow tube, much thinner than a human hair, runs through each mandible to the pointed, outer tip. Glowworm mandibles are like the fangs of a poisonous snake. When the glowworm bites into its prey, it pumps powerful poison and digestive chemicals through the hairlike tubes to the fanglike tips of the mandibles. It injects the poison through the tip of the mandibles into its victim, which quickly paralyzes it. Completely helpless and

Glowworms, like this female hanging on a blade of grass, have tremendous appetites.

Hungry glowworms crawl along the surface of a wall in search of a meal.

unable to move, the glowworm's victim can neither fight back nor escape.

After disabling its victim, the glowworm waits for the digestive chemicals to transform the victim's body tissue and muscles into a gooey liquid. The glowworm then sucks out its victim's soupy insides, leaving only an empty skin behind. It can dine on a paralyzed, but still living, earthworm for days.

Many adult firefly species never eat at all because they live for just a few days, only long enough to mate and lay eggs. Others feed on pollen and sweet nectar. Some are carnivorous, or meat eating, just as they were in the larval stage.

A Firefly-Eat-Firefly World

Sometimes fireflies are the diners. Other times they are the dinners. The females of some carnivorous species even eat their own kind. They crack the secret courting codes of other firefly species and copy them. A cannibalistic female flashes "yes" to the invitation of a courting male of another species. Her inviting glow tricks the male into thinking she will welcome him as a mate. When he lands next to her, she pounces on him and eats him alive.

After tricking him into accepting her invitation to mate, a female firefly devours a male.

Flashing Lights Say "Stay Away!"

Fireflies in all stages of life are eaten by many different kinds of

Fireflies Bulk Up

Fireflies sometimes flash their lights as a warning to predators.

predator animals, including birds, reptiles, and other kinds of insects. Fireflies use their ability to flash for protection as well as mating. Their flashing warns predators that they may be sorry if they try to make a meal out of a firefly. Poisonous chemicals in most fireflies' blood taste terrible. One mouthful convinces most predators never to feast on fireflies again.

CHAPTER 4

Fireflies Twinkle Around the World

Over many thousands of years, fireflies have been able to adapt to life in a variety of habitats all over the world, on every continent except Antarctica. They live in forests, in grassy fields, on country farms where crops are grown, and in pastures where livestock graze. They live in flower and vegetable gardens, in fruit orchards, in city parks, and in the yards of suburban houses.

Fireflies are found in different habitats throughout the world.

Because active firefly larvae spend all of their waking time and energy finding and eating food, they do not build permanent homes. They snooze wherever they find shelter—underneath logs, rotting bark, and fallen leaves on the ground, for instance. Since adult fireflies live only long enough to mate and lay eggs, they nap where it is handy and where they will not be easily discovered by predators—on the underside of a blade of grass, a tree leaf, or some other type of vegetation.

Fireflies prefer climates with mild to moderate temperatures during the summer, the season when they are active. They thrive in moist areas and are most plentiful alongside rivers and streams and near ponds, marshes, and swamps. After a rain they are often seen along roadside ditches that remain damp longer than the surrounding areas.

Southern Living

Of the 2,000 identified species of fireflies, more than 170 can be found in the United States. Most live east of the Rocky Mountains, from New York to Kansas and Georgia to Texas, and in most of the states in between. But even

Fireflies can often be found napping on the leaves of trees.

though the firefly is the official state insect of Pennsylvania, there are more of them in the southern states, because it is warmer and more humid there. Florida can claim the most fireflies for the most months of the year, because the **climate** is tropical almost all year long. In western states, sightings of fireflies are rare, but not unheard-of.

The greatest number and variety of fireflies in the world live even farther south, in the tropical climates of Central and South America and in tropical Asia. A tiny village called Kampong Kuantan, in the country of Malaysia, has become famous because it is home to one of the largest firefly colonies on the planet. Many thousands of tourists from all over

The best place to catch a jar full of fireflies in the United States is in one of the southern states.

the world visit Kampong Kuantan each year to take nighttime boat tours through swamps that are lined by mangrove trees. Masses of fireflies fill hundreds of trees. In a display that scientists cannot yet fully explain, hundreds of thousands of them wink and blink on and off at exactly the same time, all together, as if controlled by a mysterious, hidden light switch.

A few species of fireflies have even adapted to life in very arid

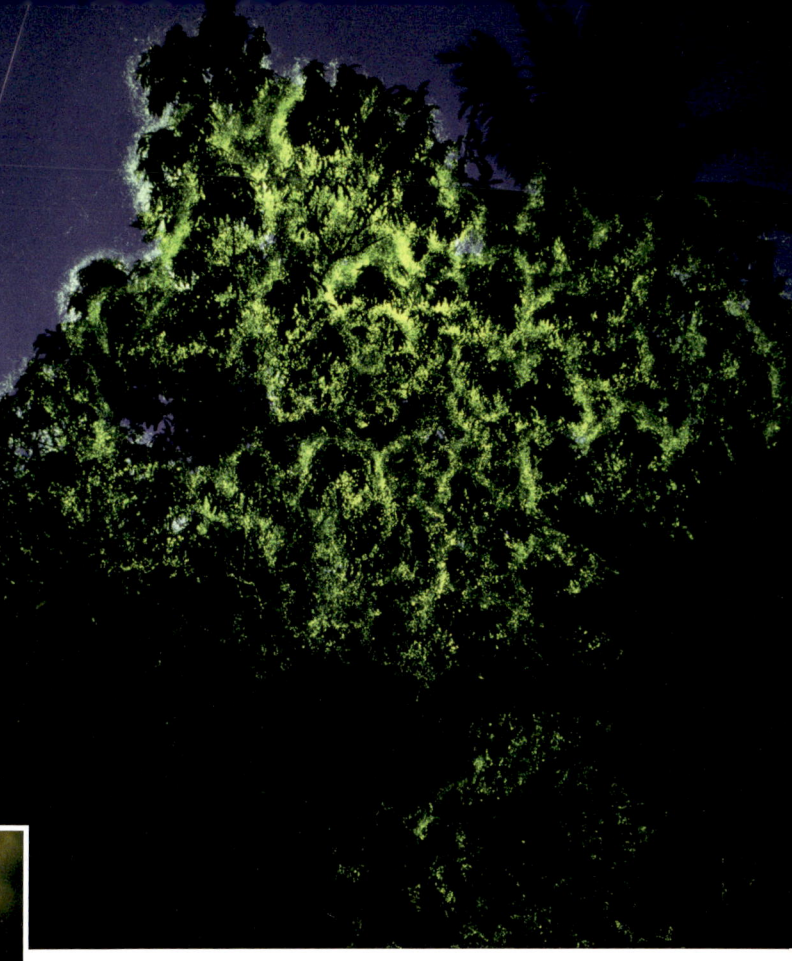

A large group of fireflies in Malaysia lights up at once, producing a magnificent glow.

parts of the world. In certain desert areas where fireflies are known to exist, the larvae and adults can be spotted only briefly, immediately following rain. Their season of light lasts no more than an hour or two.

Just a Sweet Memory

Firefly populations are dramatically declining—even disappearing—all over the world. Enormous modern cities pave over prime firefly habitat. Bold nighttime lights disturb fireflies' mating rituals. Pesticides kill the slugs, worms, and larvae that fireflies feed on and many of the fireflies themselves. Scientists predict that in many parts of the world, the magic and mystery of the firefly will soon be just a sweet memory.

Firefly populations all over the world are threatened by human activities.

GLOSSARY

antennae: Threadlike, movable feelers on the heads of insects.
bioluminescence: Light produced by living things.
climate: The average weather conditions of a place over a period of years.
courting: One insect trying to gain the cooperation of another of its species in order to mate.
cycle: A period of time taken up by a series of events that repeat themselves again and again in the same order.
luciferase: A special enzyme in the firefly's body that combines with luciferin to make bioluminescence possible.
luciferin: A rare chemical in the firefly's body that combines with luciferase to create light.
luminous: Glowing.
mandibles: The first pair of an insect's mouth parts that form biting organs.
mating: A male and female of a species joining to produce young.
metamorphosis: The distinct changes an insect undergoes from egg to larva to pupa to adult.
organs: Parts of a person, animal, or plant that are specialized to do a particular task.
species: A category of living things of the same, distinct kind that are able to reproduce with one another.
transformation: A complete change.

FOR FURTHER EXPLORATION

Books

Sneed B. Collard, *A Firefly Biologist at Work.* New York: Franklin Watts, 2001. This book follows the footsteps of biologist Jim Case as he travels thousands of miles to Malaysia to study one of the largest firefly populations in the world.

Louise Dyer Harris and Norman Dyer, *Flash: The Life Story of a Firefly.* Boston: Little, Brown, 1966. This story of a firefly named Flash records in great detail an average day in the life of a firefly.

Judith Janda Presnall, *Animals That Glow.* New York: Franklin Watts, 1993. This book is an illustrated study of insects that are bioluminescent, including fireflies and glowworms.

Web Sites

Animal Planet: Corwin's Carnival of Creatures (www.animal.discovery.com/fansites/jeffcorwin/carnival/crawler/firefly.html). Information on habitat, diet, and life cycle of fireflies.

Insects in the Wet Tropics (www.wettropics.gov.au/pa/pa_fireflies.html). Information on fireflies and bioluminescence in fireflies and other animals.

Norman Bird Sanctuary (www.normanbirdsanctuary.org/artman/publish/article_43.shtml). Photographs and lots of information on all aspects of fireflies, with an emphasis on their decreasing numbers throughout the world.

Ohio State University Extension Fact Sheet/Entomology (www.ohioline.osu.edu/hygfact/2000/2125.html). Photographs, firefly myths, information on how fireflies are used in scientific research for disease cures, and how bioluminescence works.

World Kids (www.worldkids.net/critters/QnA/messages/409.html). Frequently asked questions and answers and a message board for additional questions and exchanging information about fireflies.

INDEX

abdomen, 8
adult
  body of, 6, 8
  food of, 18–19
antennae, 6
Asia, 24–25

bioluminescence, 9
blinking. *See* flashing
body
  of adult, 6, 8
  of larvae, 12–13, 17
breathing, 8

Central America, 24
colors, 6
courting, 8

eggs, 8, 11–12
elytra, 6
eyes, 6

flashing, 5
  of desert fireflies, 26
  for hunting, 19
  for mating, 8–9
  for protection, 20
Florida, 24

glowworms. *See* larvae

habitats, 21–26
head, 6
homes, 22

Kampong Kuantan Malaysia), 24–25

larvae, 12–14, 16–19
legs, 6
life cycle
  eggs, 8, 11–12
  larvae, 12–14, 16–19
  mating, 6, 8–9, 11
  pupae, 14–15
life span, 22
lights, artificial, 26
luciferase, 9
luciferin, 9

Malaysia, 24–25
mandibles, 6, 17
mating, 6, 8–9, 11

Pennsylvania, 24
pesticides, 26
poisons, 17–18
predators
  adults as, 18–19
  of fireflies, 19–20
  larvae as, 16–19
pupae, 14–15

senses, 6, 17
South America, 24
species, 5, 8–9, 23
spiracles, 8

thorax, 6
threats, 19–20, 26
tourism, 24–25

wings, 6, 8

of fireflies, with an emphasis on their decreasing numbers throughout the world.

Ohio State University Extension Fact Sheet/Entomology (www.ohioline.osu.edu/hygfact/2000/2125.html). Photographs, firefly myths, information on how fireflies are used in scientific research for disease cures, and how bioluminescence works.

World Kids (www.worldkids.net/critters/QnA/messages/409.html). Frequently asked questions and answers and a message board for additional questions and exchanging information about fireflies.

INDEX

abdomen, 8
adult
  body of, 6, 8
  food of, 18–19
antennae, 6
Asia, 24–25

bioluminescence, 9
blinking. *See* flashing
body
  of adult, 6, 8
  of larvae, 12–13, 17
breathing, 8

Central America, 24
colors, 6
courting, 8

eggs, 8, 11–12
elytra, 6
eyes, 6

flashing, 5
  of desert fireflies, 26
  for hunting, 19
  for mating, 8–9
  for protection, 20
Florida, 24

glowworms. *See* larvae

habitats, 21–26
head, 6
homes, 22

Kampong Kuantan Malaysia), 24–25

larvae, 12–14, 16–19
legs, 6
life cycle
  eggs, 8, 11–12
  larvae, 12–14, 16–19
  mating, 6, 8–9, 11
  pupae, 14–15
life span, 22
lights, artificial, 26
luciferase, 9
luciferin, 9

Malaysia, 24–25
mandibles, 6, 17
mating, 6, 8–9, 11

Pennsylvania, 24
pesticides, 26
poisons, 17–18
predators
  adults as, 18–19
  of fireflies, 19–20
  larvae as, 16–19
pupae, 14–15

senses, 6, 17
South America, 24
species, 5, 8–9, 23
spiracles, 8

thorax, 6
threats, 19–20, 26
tourism, 24–25

wings, 6, 8

PICTURE CREDITS

Cover: Darwin Dale/Photo Researchers, Inc.
© AP/Wide World Photos, 19 (right)
© Bill Beatty/Visuals Unlimited, 20
Scott Camazine/Photo Researchers, Inc., 26
© B. Borrell Casals; Frank Lane Picture Agency/CORBIS, 6
© Mark Cassino/SuperStock, 7, 19 (left)
Stephen Dalton/Photo Researchers, Inc., 17
© Jeff Daly/Visuals Unlimited, 4, 23, 24, 25 (left)
© Michael Durham/Visuals Unlimited, 13
© Frank Lane Picture Agency/CORBIS, 12
© Eric and David Hosking/CORBIS, 14
© Mitsuhiko Imamori/Minden Pictures, 9, 22, 25 (right)
© Adam Jones/Visuals Unlimited, 15
Keith Kent/Photo Researchers, Inc., 10
Steve Percival/Photo Researchers, Inc., 18
Dr. Paul A. Zahl/Photo Researchers, Inc., 8

ABOUT THE AUTHOR

Lynn Kuntz is an award-winning writer whose nonfiction children's books include: *The Naturalist's Handbook, Activities for Young Explorers, American Grub, Eats for Kids from All Fifty States*, (cowritten with Jan Fleming), and *The Roman Colosseum* in the KidHaven Press Great Structures in History series. Kuntz has written newspaper and magazine fiction and nonfiction, five award-winning films for children, and one feature family film, *Dakota*. Kuntz has received a number of awards, including a Dallas Press Club Award for Outstanding Achievement in Journalism and the Colorado Author's League Best Children's Book of the Year Award. She teaches writing for children in the Extended Studies Program at Fort Lewis College. Kuntz, the mother of four children, lives in Colorado and loves to ski, hike, and ride horses in the mountains.

J 595.7644 KUN
Kuntz, Lynn, 1953-
Firefly

4-28-08

WATCHUNG LIBRARY
12 STIRLING ROAD
WATCHUNG, NJ 07069